Colorado

Jim Ollhoff

Visit us at
www.abdopublishing.com

Published by ABDO Publishing Company, 8000 West 78th Street, Suite 310, Edina, Minnesota 55439 USA. Copyright ©2010 by Abdo Consulting Group, Inc. International copyrights reserved in all countries. No part of this book may be reproduced in any form without written permission from the publisher. The Checkerboard Library™ is a trademark and logo of ABDO Publishing Company.

Printed in the United States.

Editor: John Hamilton
Graphic Design: Sue Hamilton
Cover Illustration: Neil Klinepier
Cover Photo: iStock Photo
Interior Photo Credits: Alamy, AP Images, Colorado Department of Transportation, Colorado Geological Survey, Comstock, Corbis, David Jolley, David Olson, Getty, Granger Collection, iStock Photo, John Hamilton, Library of Congress, Metro-Goldwyn-Mayer Studios, Mile High Maps, Mountain High Maps, North Wind Picture Archives, One Mile Up, Red Rocks Park, Rick Kimpel, and Wikimedia.
Statistics: State population statistics taken from 2008 U.S. Census Bureau estimates. City and town population statistics taken from July 1, 2007, U.S. Census Bureau estimates. Land and water area statistics taken from 2000 Census, U.S. Census Bureau.

Library of Congress Cataloging-in-Publication Data

Ollhoff, Jim, 1959-
  Colorado / Jim Ollhoff.
      p. cm. -- (The United States)
  Includes index.
  ISBN 978-1-60453-641-6
  1. Colorado--Juvenile literature. I. Title.

F776.3.O44 2010
978.8--dc22

                      2008051026

Table of Contents

Centennial State

Colorado residents have many reasons to love their state, including plenty of space, lots of minerals, good soil, and incredible beauty. The Rocky Mountains cover about half of Colorado.

Colorado has had a rich heritage with many different cultures. The Cheyenne, Arapaho, and Ute tribes made Colorado their home for generations. Because Colorado was a Spanish territory for many years, some of its cities have Spanish names. Folktales, music, and food have been influenced by these different cultures.

Colorado became a state in 1876, 100 years after the United States became its own country. In memory of this important time, Colorado is known as the "Centennial State." Centennial means 100 years.

Sunrise at Colorado's
Uncompahgre National Forest.

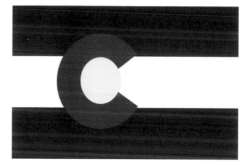

Quick Facts

Name: Colorado is from a Spanish word meaning "colored red."

State Capital: Denver

Date of Statehood: August 1, 1876 (38th state)

Population: 4,939,456 (22nd-most populous state)

Area (Total Land and Water): 104,094 square miles (269,602 sq km), 8th-largest state

Largest City: Denver, population 588,349

Nickname: The Centennial State

Motto: *Nil Sine Numine* (Nothing Without the Deity)

State Bird: Lark Bunting

Columbine

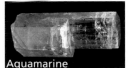
Aquamarine

Blue Spruce

Mount Elbert

CO Low Point

State Flower: White and Lavender Columbine

State Gemstone: Aquamarine

State Tree: Colorado Blue Spruce

State Songs: "Where the Columbines Grow" and "Rocky Mountain High"

Highest Point: Mount Elbert, 14,433 feet (4,399 m)

Lowest Point: 3,315 ft (1,010 m) on the Arikaree River

Average July Temperature: 70°F (21°C)

Record High Temperature: 118°F (48°C) on July 11, 1888 at Bennett

Average January Temperature: 15° (-9°C)

Record Low Temperature: -61°F (-52°C) on February 1, 1985, at Maybell

Average Annual Precipitation: 15 inches (38 cm)

Number of U.S. Senators: 2

Number of U.S. Representatives: 7

U.S. Postal Service Abbreviation: CO

Geography

   Colorado can be divided into three areas. These are the plains, the mountains, and the Colorado Piedmont.

   The east side of the state is plains. This means it is mostly flat, with some low rolling hills. Much of this area lacks moisture. There is less farming in Colorado than in other states. Much of the land is used for cattle grazing.

   On the west side of the state are the mountains. The name of this area is the Southern Rocky Mountains. They are very high mountains, with deep canyons. There are more than 800 mountaintops that are over 11,000 feet (3,353 m) high. There are high plateaus, too. A plateau is a large, flat area that is higher than the area around it.

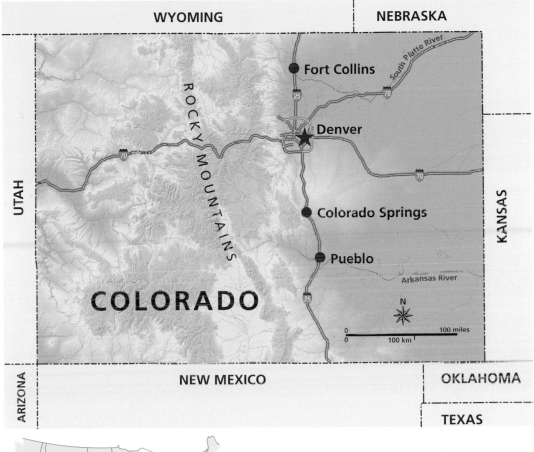

WYOMING

NEBRASKA

Fort Collins

South Platte River

25

76

Denver

70

UTAH

Colorado Springs

KANSAS

Pueblo

Arkansas River

ROCKY MOUNTAINS

COLORADO

N

25

0   100 miles
0   100 km

ARIZONA

NEW MEXICO

OKLAHOMA

TEXAS

Colorado's total land and water area is 104,094 square miles (269,602 sq km). It is the 8th-largest state. The state capital is Denver.

In the middle of the state is a long narrow strip of land going north and south. This strip of land separates the mountains from the plains. It is called the foothills or the Colorado Piedmont. Most people who live in Colorado live in the Piedmont region. The cities of Denver,

The Colorado Piedmont is a hilly area at the base of the Rocky Mountains.

Boulder, Colorado Springs, Pueblo, and others lie on this narrow strip of land. People like living there because water is easily available. These foothills also have a good climate and are close to Colorado's beautiful mountains.

Although many of Colorado's rivers are dry much of the year, a few major rivers flow. The Arkansas River runs through the southern part of the state. The South Platte River flows in the northern part of the state.

The South Platte River runs through Denver, Colorado.

Climate and Weather

On Colorado's eastern plains, the summer average is about 75 degrees Fahrenheit (24°C). Temperatures can get above 100 degrees Fahrenheit (38°C). The winters are cold and dry in this area. It can be windy, too, since there are no mountains on the eastern plains. Average January temperature on the plains is a cold 10 to 30 degrees Fahrenheit (-12° to -1°C).

On the west side of the state, there are a lot of differences in temperature and precipitation. Weather in one place can be different than the weather just a few miles away. This is because of how the air moves through the mountains' high elevations.

Mountain temperatures in July might average 60 degrees Fahrenheit (16°C). Valleys can be much warmer.

In January, temperatures might get to 17 degrees Fahrenheit (-8°C). But, at very high elevations, temperatures can get as cold as -50 degrees Fahrenheit (-46°C).

A plow clears heavy snow from a Colorado road.

Plants and Animals

The plains of eastern Colorado are covered in short, prairie grasses. Prairie dogs, chipmunks, and jackrabbits make their homes on the flat lands. Common birds include the lark bunting and the meadowlark.

Ground Squirrel

There are forests in the mountains and high plateaus. Douglas fir, blue spruce, Englemann spruce, and aspen are common trees. When the mountains get very high, over 11,500 feet (3,505 m), there are no longer trees. This is known as the tree line. Mosses and small plants are the only vegetation at very high elevations.

Bald eagles are found mainly in the mountains. Some have been found in the northeast corner of the state.

Bald eagles are found near Colorado's mountains.

In the mountains, there are many big animals. Deer, elk, coyotes, bobcats, and mountain lions are seen in these high elevations. Smaller animals, such as muskrats and beavers, find food in the mountains. During winter, many of the animals move to the valleys or lower elevations where it is warmer.

The Rocky Mountain bighorn sheep is the state animal of Colorado. It is found in the mountains. The males are called rams. They are famous for their big, curled horns. Sometimes they fight each other. Loud crashes echo across the area when they bang their horns together. Adult bighorns can weigh 117 to 279 pounds (53 to 127 kg).

Bighorn Rams

A Colorado mountain lion.

Coyote

Mule Deer

Bull Elk

History

People have been in Colorado for thousands of years. North of Denver is an archeological site where tools have been found that are 13,000 years old.

The ancient Pueblo people, sometimes called the Anasazi, lived in the southwest corner of the state. They came to the area about 100 AD and perhaps much earlier.

The Anasazi lived in the cliffs of southwest Colorado.

They built multi-level buildings in the cliffs. Many of their homes can still be seen in Mesa Verde National Park. In about 1300 AD, the ancient Pueblo people vanished from the area. They may have moved farther southwest to escape a long period of dry weather.

The Anasazi built Cliff Palace between 1190 and 1280 AD. It was home to about 100 people. Today it is part of Mesa Verde National Park.

In the early 1500s, the Spanish claimed Mexico. They also claimed lands to the north of Mexico, all the way to the Arkansas River in Colorado. The Spanish conquistadors may have explored the southern part of Colorado, looking for gold. Of course, Native Americans already lived there. The Arapaho and the Cheyenne lived in the plains, on the east side of the state. The Ute tribe lived in the Rocky Mountains.

Members of the Colorado Ute tribe in 1913.

In 1801, the French acquired land west of the Mississippi from Spain. In 1803, the United States bought the middle section of North America from France. This was called the Louisiana Purchase. This purchase included a large section of Colorado.

One of the first Europeans to explore Colorado was James Pursley, a fur trader. He came through in 1804. In 1806, Zebulon Pike explored Colorado.

Zebulon Pike explored Colorado's Rocky Mountain area in 1806.

Bent's Fort trading post provided shelter and supplies for trappers and traders.

Stephen Long led an expedition to explore Colorado in 1820. Fur trappers and traders also came to the state during this time. In the early 1830s, Bent's Fort and Fort St. Vrain were built to give shelter and provide supplies to the fur traders. In the 1840s, John Fremont and Kit Carson explored Colorado's mountain passes.

Excitement in the area exploded with the discovery of gold in 1858 and 1859. Thousands of treasure hunters rushed to the towns of Cherry Creek, Gold Hill, Black Hawk, Central City, and others. This was the first big arrival of Europeans to Colorado.

Because of the huge rush of people to find gold, there were food shortages. People began to farm the land. They used water from rivers to irrigate their fields. Agriculture developed and grew to be an important business in the state.

Colorado was organized as a territory in 1861. Fifteen years later, it was admitted as the 38th state in the United States.

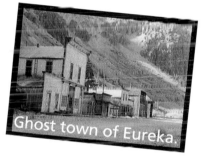
Ghost town of Eureka.

By the 1890s, many of the gold mines closed. Ghost towns dotted the state. Farmers began to raise cattle and sheep. Livestock grazed in the open spaces.

During World War II (1939-1945), Americans feared that the enemy would attack the coasts of the United States. Colorado's inland location seemed safe. Large military bases were built in Colorado. After the war, leaders made Colorado's military bases even larger.

Did You Know?

Colorado has a military base built *inside* one of its mountains. It is called the Cheyenne Mountain Complex. It is part of the North American Aerospace Defense Command, or NORAD.

The entry to the Cheyenne Mountain Complex.

Beginning in the 1950s, the United States and the Soviet Union were in conflict with each other. Although there was no fighting, both countries were afraid the other nation would attack them.

If Soviet missiles were launched, the United States wanted a military base that

Inside the Cheyenne Mountain Complex.

could track these weapons. Military leaders also wanted a place that could withstand a missile attack. The base was built inside Cheyenne Mountain in Colorado Springs.

Today, the military is not as worried about a missile attack. The main operations have been moved to Peterson Air Force Base in Colorado Springs. This base is also the location of the Air Force Space Command.

People

Lon Chaney in his role in *London After Midnight.*

Lon Chaney (1883-1930) was one of early film's most famous actors. Born in Colorado Springs, his parents were deaf and unable to speak. He learned to "talk" by acting out his words. He starred in many silent movies. He was known for his roles in horror films. *The Hunchback of Notre Dame* (1923) and *The Phantom of the Opera* (1925) were two of his most famous silent movies. Chaney died shortly after his first talking movie was released.

Boxer **Jack Dempsey** (1895-1983) was born in Manassa, Colorado. Dempsey started boxing in 1914. He became one of the greatest boxers of all time. He held the title of American World Heavyweight Boxing Champion from 1919 to 1926. He served in the Coast Guard during World War II. After

Jack Dempsey became one of the greatest boxers of all time.

retiring from boxing, he opened a restaurant in New York City. Dempsey also wrote or co-wrote several books, including one about his own life.

Singer and songwriter **John Denver** (1943-1997) was born in New Mexico. His parents named him Henry John Deutschendorf, Jr. By the mid-1960s, he adopted the name of John Denver, after the capital of the state he loved. He became one of the most popular singers of the 1970s. One of his most famous songs  was "Rocky Mountain High," named for Colorado. This became one of Colorado's official state songs. Denver was an experienced pilot. Sadly, he died when the experimental plane he was flying crashed into the ocean.

Chief Ouray (1833?-1880) was a chief of the Ute tribe of Colorado. His name means "the arrow." Ouray learned to speak English, Spanish, and Apache, which helped him make treaties with other nations. He tried to find peaceful solutions for problems between European settlers and the Ute. President Rutherford B. Hayes called Chief Ouray "the most intelligent man I've ever conversed with." The town of Ouray, Colorado, is named in honor of the wise Ute leader.

Cities

Denver is the capital of Colorado. It has 588,349 people. When all of the people in the surrounding cities are counted, the population is almost three million. The city's elevation is 5,280 feet (1,609 m) above sea level. Since 5,280 feet is the same amount of feet in a mile, it has the nickname "the mile-high city." The area had long been a place where Arapaho Indians and fur traders lived. When gold was discovered nearby in 1858, people rushed in. Denver became the state capital in 1876.

The city of **Colorado Springs** sits near the base of Pikes Peak. This mountain is in the Front Range of the Rocky Mountains. Colorado Springs has a population of 376,427. The city is the home of the University of Colorado, as well as other colleges. Nearby is the Garden of the Gods, a famous natural park. Large military installations are based in and around Colorado Springs.

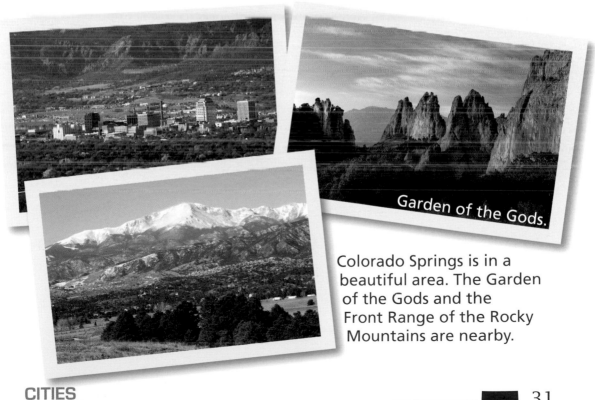

Garden of the Gods.

Colorado Springs is in a beautiful area. The Garden of the Gods and the Front Range of the Rocky Mountains are nearby.

Old Town Square street corner in Fort Collins, Colorado.

The city of **Fort Collins** began as a U.S. Army fort in 1864. It was meant to be a stopping point for travelers on the Overland Trail. It also provided protection for the mail routes. Settlers came to the area to farm in the 1870s. Today, the population is 133,899. It is the home of Colorado State University, as well as other colleges.

Pueblo is about 100 miles (161 km) south of Denver. It has a population of 103,805. It began in the 1840s as a trading post called Fort Pueblo. The discovery of gold in Colorado in the late 1850s brought many settlers to the area.

The Arkansas River runs through Pueblo, Colorado.

Transportation

Two main interstate highways go across the state. Interstate 25 goes north and south, through the cities of Fort Collins, Denver, Colorado Springs, and Pueblo. Interstate 25 roughly follows the foothills, so the mountains are to the west of I-25 and the plains are to the east. Interstate 70 runs through Denver. It then heads west through the mountains and east to Kansas. A shorter interstate highway, I-76, comes down from Nebraska and ends in Denver.

About 60 miles (97 km) west of Denver, there is a long tunnel through a mountain. It is called the Eisenhower Memorial Tunnel. Construction on it was finished in 1973. It is nearly 2 miles (3 km) long.

Eisenhower Memorial Tunnel

Denver International Airport is one of the main airports in the nation. It covers almost 53 square miles (137 sq km). Completed in 1995, the airport can handle 50 million passengers a year.

Controllers in the main tower at Denver International Airport.

Natural Resources

Agriculture has always been important to Colorado, even though a lot of the state gets little rain. Much of Colorado's land is irrigated. This means that pipes bring in water to wet down the fields. Farmers grow millet, corn, sunflowers, potatoes, hay, and wheat. There are also many

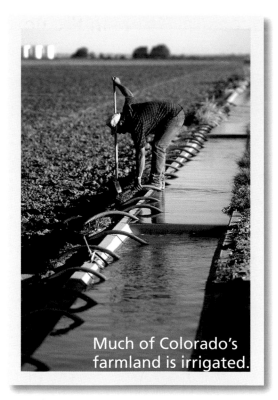

Much of Colorado's farmland is irrigated.

ranches in Colorado, with almost three million cattle. Farmers raise chickens and dairy cows, too.

One hundred years ago, Colorado was heavily mined. Today, the mining of coal, oil, sand, and gravel are still important to the state. There are also large deposits of coal in the northwest part of the state that have not yet been mined.

A coal train in western Colorado.

Industry

Manufacturing, agriculture, and tourism are three big sources of money for the state.

Tourism brings in a huge amount of money. Colorado is famous for winter sports, such as skiing. Black Canyon of the Gunnison, Great Sand Dunes, Mesa Verde, and Rocky Mountain are national parks that bring many visitors to the state.

Machinery, wood and paper products, and military equipment are manufactured in Colorado. There are 30,500 farms and ranches in the state.

The federal government is one of the major employers in Colorado. There are a number of military bases and government facilities in the state. Colorado has many scientific businesses and high-tech industries.

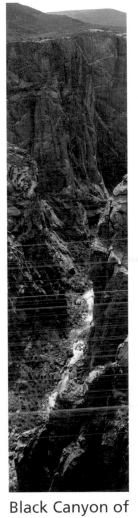

Black Canyon of
the Gunnison
National Park.

Great
Sand Dunes
National Park.

Mesa Verde
National
Park.

Rocky
Mountain
National Park.

Sports

Colorado is able to support many professional sports teams. The Colorado Rockies play Major League Baseball. The Denver Broncos play in the National Football League, and have won two Super Bowls. The Colorado Avalanche play in the National Hockey League, and the Denver Nuggets play in the National Basketball Association.

Colorado has professional teams in other sports as well. There are soccer, lacrosse, and arena football teams that compete professionally.

Outdoor recreation is popular in Colorado. Canoeing, backpacking, mountain climbing, hunting, and wildlife viewing are great pastimes in the state. Winter activities include skiing, snowmobiling, and snowshoeing. The adventurous enjoy whitewater rafting and hang gliding.

Entertainment

There are many opportunities for entertainment and arts in Colorado. The Denver Zoo is one of the most popular attractions. It was founded in 1896, and covers 80 acres (32 ha).

Red Rocks Park is a large, outdoor, natural theater. It is west of Denver and hosts musical events.

A silverback gorilla at the Denver Zoo.

An evening concert at Red Rocks Park.

There are many art museums, including the Denver Art Museum, the Colorado Springs Fine Arts Center, the Aspen Art Museum, and the Kirkland Museum in Denver.

Colorado is also a good place for history. The state's historical society has a museum in Denver. There are also many historical forts and buildings throughout the state. Many have been restored so that they look like they did generations ago.

The Ghost Town Museum of Colorado Springs is an Old West town built from the buildings left after the Pikes Peak gold mining era.

Timeline

1300—A long drought, or perhaps fighting with other tribes, forces the ancient Pueblo people to leave their homes in Mesa Verde.

1776—Fathers Escalante and Dominguez seek a route to California. They may have traveled through Colorado.

1803—The United States buys land from France. The Louisiana Purchase includes much of Colorado.

1804-1825—Frontiersmen, scouts, and fur traders explore Colorado.

1832—Bent's Fort, an important trading post, is built.

1858-1859—Gold is discovered in several places in Colorado.

1870—Railroads connect Denver and Cheyenne, Wyoming.

1877—The University of Colorado begins classes.

1941-1945—During World War II, the U.S. military builds several bases.

2001—Colorado Avalanche wins the National Hockey League Stanley Cup Championship.

Glossary

Anasazi—Sometimes called the ancient Pueblo people. They lived in the southwestern United States, including an area of Colorado, until about 1300 AD. They built their homes in the cliffs.

Arapaho—A Native American tribe that lived on the eastern plains of Colorado before the Europeans came.

Cheyenne—A Native American tribe that lived on the eastern plains of Colorado before the Europeans came.

Conquistadors—Spanish soldiers and explorers who came over to the Americas in the 1500s. They used force to conquer native people and take control of their lands.

Foothills—Small hills where the land of the plains begins to rise into mountains.

Louisiana Purchase—The purchase by the United States of about 530 million acres (214 million ha) of land from France in 1803.

Piedmont—A long narrow strip of land in Colorado going north and south, between the mountains and the plains.

Plateau—A large, flat section of land that is higher than the area around it.

Silent Movies—Movies before movies had sound.

Soviet Union—Today, the country of Russia and a number of surrounding countries.

Ute—A Native American tribe that lived in the mountains of Colorado before the Europeans came.

World War II—A conflict across the world, lasting from 1939-1945. The United States entered the war in December 1941.

Index